I0414005

To my family, thank you for always bringing out the best in me.

Printed in the United States of America

HOW IT WORKS:

1. GRAB YOUR FAVORITE CRAYONS, PENCILS, GEL PENS AND COLOR HOW YOU WOULD LIKE. STAY IN THE LINES OR OUTSIDE!

2. THERE IS A BLANK PAGE BETWEEN EACH SECTION TO PROTECT THE PREVIOUS PAGE AND FOR YOU TO TEST OUT YOUR COLORS.

3. THE MINI DRAWINGS ARE GREAT TO GIVE TO FRIENDS, FAMILY AND TO KEEP ON YOUR WALLS AS A CUT OUT MINI POSTER. ENJOY!

WITH LOVE,
KIMBERLY FAYE

SEEK TO BE WORTH KNOWING
RATHER THAN TO BE
WELL KNOWN.

SEEK TO BE WORTH KNOWING
RATHER THAN TO BE
WELL KNOWN.

SEEK TO BE WORTH KNOWING
RATHER THAN TO BE
WELL KNOWN.

WHEN YOU FEEL LIKE
QUITTING.
REMEMBER WHY
YOU STARTED.

YOU ARE A UNIQUE FLOWER.
THERE IS NO COMPARISON.

YOU ARE A UNIQUE FLOWER.
THERE IS NO COMPARISON.

YOU ARE A UNIQUE FLOWER.
THERE IS NO COMPARISON.

IF YOU STUMBLE
MAKE IT PART
THE DANCE

START EACH DAY

WITH A GRATEFUL HEART

START EACH DAY

WITH A GRATEFUL HEART

START EACH DAY

WITH A GRATEFUL HEART

NOBODY IN THE WORLD IS YOU

AND THAT IS YOUR SUPER POWER

NOBODY IN THE WORLD IS YOU

AND THAT IS YOUR SUPER POWER

NOBODY IN THE WORLD IS YOU

AND THAT IS YOUR SUPER POWER

NOBODY IN THE WORLD IS YOU

DO SOMETHING TODAY

THAT YOUR FUTURE SELF
WILL THANK YOU FOR

WHOEVER TRIES TO BRING YOU DOWN, IS ALREADY BELOW YOU.

DO SOMETHING TODAY

THAT YOUR FUTURE SELF WILL THANK YOU FOR

DO SOMETHING TODAY

THAT YOUR FUTURE SELF WILL THANK YOU FOR

WHOEVER TRIES TO BRING YOU DOWN, IS ALREADY BELOW YOU.

MAKE YOURSELF A PRIORITY

YOU ARE YOUR LONGEST COMMITMENT

MAKE YOURSELF A PRIORITY

YOU ARE YOUR LONGEST COMMITMENT

MAKE YOURSELF A PRIORITY

YOU ARE YOUR LONGEST COMMITMENT

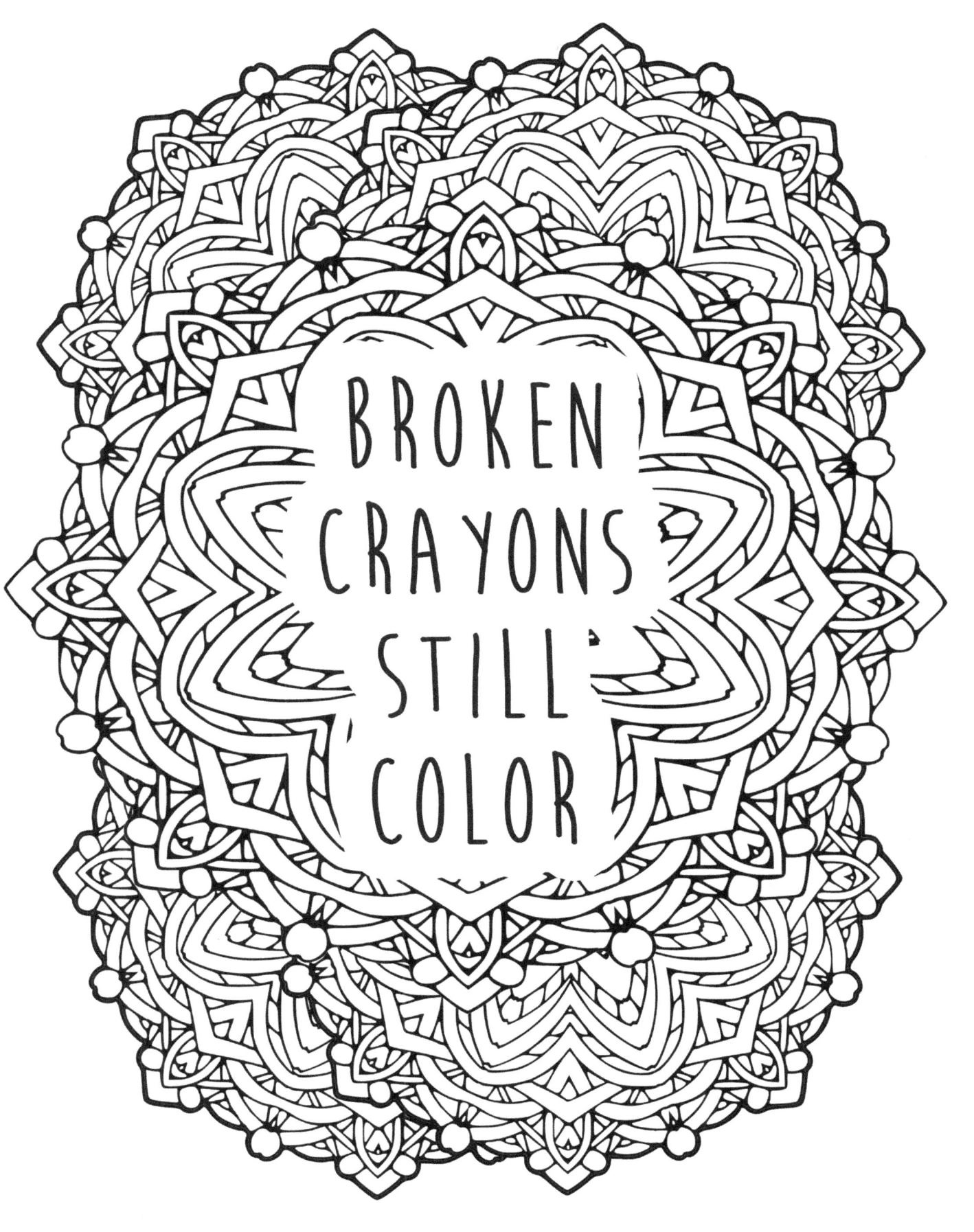

BREATHE
IN AND
OUT

A LITTLE PROGRESS

EACH DAY

ADDS UP TO BIG RESULTS

A LITTLE PROGRESS

EACH DAY

ADDS UP TO BIG RESULTS

A LITTLE PROGRESS

EACH DAY

ADDS UP TO BIG RESULTS

YOUR ATTITUDE DETERMINES YOUR ALTITUDE IN LIFE.

YOUR ATTITUDE DETERMINES YOUR ALTITUDE IN LIFE.

YOUR ATTITUDE DETERMINES YOUR ALTITUDE IN LIFE.